Animales del zoológico / Zoo Animals

JIRAFAS / GIRAFFES AT THE ZOO

By Finn Ward
Traducido por Ana María García

Gareth Stevens
PUBLISHING

Please visit our website, www.garethstevens.com. For a free color catalog of all our high-quality books, call toll free 1-800-542-2595 or fax 1-877-542-2596.

Library of Congress Cataloging-in-Publication Data

Ward, Finn.
Giraffes at the zoo = Jirafas / Finn Ward.
pages cm. — (Zoo animals = Animales del zoológico)
Parallel title: Animales del zoológico.
In English and Spanish.
Includes index.
ISBN 978-1-4824-3229-9 (library binding)
1. Giraffe—Juvenile literature. 2. Zoo animals—Juvenile literature. I. Title.
SF408.6.G57W37 2016
599.638—dc23

First Edition

Published in 2016 by
Gareth Stevens Publishing
111 East 14th Street, Suite 349
New York, NY 10003

Editor: Ryan Nagelhout
Designer: Katelyn E. Reynolds

Photo credits: Cover, p. 1 Phongkrit/Shutterstock.com; p. 5 Nadia Borisevich/Shutterstock.com; p. 7 Diola/Shutterstock.com; p. 9 sevenke/Shutterstock.com; pp. 11, 13, 24 (neck) Evgeniya Uvarova/Shutterstock.com; pp. 15, 24 (spot) Peter O'Toole/Shutterstock.com; p. 17 Julia Xanthos/NY Daily News Archive/Getty Images; pp. 19, 24 (leaves) ilovezion/Shutterstock.com; p. 21 Thitisan/Shutterstock.com; p. 23 Joy Brown/Shutterstock.com.

Printed in the United States of America

CPSIA compliance information: Batch #CS15GS: For further information contact Gareth Stevens, New York, New York at 1-800-542-2595.

Contenido

Contents

El zoológico está
lleno de animales.

The zoo is full
of animals.

¡En el zoológico viven algunas jirafas!

Giraffes live at the zoo!

Caminan en cuatro patas.

They walk on four legs.

Tienen el cuello largo.

They have long necks.

Les gusta vivir
en grupo.

They like to live
in groups.

Las jirafas tienen
mucho pelo.
El pelo tiene manchas
de color marrón.

Giraffes have lots of hair.
It has brown spots on it.

En los zoológicos
las cuidan.

Zoos take care of them.

A las jirafas les
encanta comer hojas.

Giraffes love
to eat leaves.

¡En algunos zoológicos puedes darles de comer!

Some zoos let you feed them!

Los bebés jirafa
son preciosos.
Son sus crías.

Baby giraffes are cute.
They are called calves.

Palabras que debes aprender/ Words to Know

(las) hojas/
leaves

(el) cuello/
neck

(la) mancha/
spot

Índice/Index